Blak

SETTING UP AND RUNNING A SUCCESSFUL HOME BUSINESS

Kelvin Worthington

PASCAL
PRESS

ISBN 1 74125 149 4

Pascal Press
PO Box 250
Glebe NSW 2037
(02) 8585 4044
www.pascalpress.com.au

Publisher: Vivienne Petris Joannou
Project editor: Ian Rohr
Editor: Jo Avigdor
Page design, layout and cover by DiZign Pty Ltd
Photos by Photos.com, Photodisc
Printed in Australia by Printing Creations

A NOTE FROM THE PUBLISHER

The idea of working from home, of running your own business and being your own boss, is very appealing to many Australians. And, with the rapid advances we have seen in technology, it is becoming more and more 'do-able'. This Go Guide takes you through the many issues that you need to consider before launching a home business – from the planning to the practical to the personal, legal and financial. Packed with useful information and handy tips it will help you weigh up your options when it comes to the weighty decision of setting up and running your own home business.

As with all our Go Guides we aim to bring you the most useful information in the least number of pages — who has time to read lengthy books? This book will give you quick access to the information, ideas and skills you need to know without the padding contained in so many self-help books.

If you have any comments on how this book could be improved, please do not hesitate to email me at matthew@pascalpress.com.au.

Matthew Blake
Publisher

ABOUT THE AUTHOR

Kelvin Worthington has over 25 years experience in business banking, both in the UK and Australia. He was a Small Business Advisor for a major UK bank and a volunteer Business Mentor with the Princes Youth Business Trust, a charitable organisation which helps young people establish and run their own business. He currently runs his own consultancy advising clients on setting up and running a business.

Kelvin has an Honours degree in financial services from the University of Central England focusing on strategic management, marketing, management of company finance, accounting, strategic management of IT, statistics, decision techniques and quantitative methods. He is an Associate of the Chartered Institute of Bankers (London).

TABLE OF CONTENTS

INTRODUCTION

Many small or home businesses do not survive to their third birthday. This is a sad but true fact. The aim of this Guide is to provide **practical, easy-to-understand** help for you to set up and run a successful home business.

While establishing your own business can be a daunting prospect, it can also bring great **personal satisfaction, independence** and the freedom of being your own boss. It also allows you the flexibility to manage the business **around your lifestyle** and provides, hopefully, a **financial reward**. Talk to any person running their own home business and you will find that some, if not all, of these incentives motivated them to leave the security of a paid position with an employer.

Setting up your own business involves **taking an idea and developing it into a viable business**. It requires courage, vision, energy, enthusiasm and focus for your idea to evolve into a successful business. This Guide seeks to help you navigate that journey by setting out some **basic steps** including the development of a **Business Plan** which, if followed, will provide a firm foundation for a successful home business.

In starting this journey it is absolutely vital to have the **support of your family**. Discuss your ideas with them and the personal and financial consequences which will come with running your own home business. Keep them informed as the business progresses, so that they can share in the ups and downs and provide practical and emotional support as the business moves forward.

A number of issues are common to all new small businesses. However, if you are going to operate your business from home you will need to consider a range of **additional challenges** which this Guide will take you through. I sincerely hope that the information it contains will help ensure your home business is a long-term success far beyond its third birthday!

RUNNING A BUSINESS FROM HOME

Operating a business from home is in some ways very different from operating a business from an office, factory or shop. It is important to think about the following **advantages and disadvantages** in terms of your own personal financial and family situation as well as your individual personality and temperament.

Advantages

Flexible lifestyle

One of the main reasons people choose to set up and run their own home business is **lifestyle**. Perhaps the major attraction is that working from home allows **greater flexibility in managing work and family responsibilities**. Many people today are seeking ways to spend more time with their families, particularly if they have young children. When you work from home, you can take time out of work during the day to spend some with the family or attend a school function. Once the children have gone to bed you can settle down to some work.

Another big attraction for many people is that they no longer have to travel to and from a place of work. They are **freed from the stress of commuting** with overcrowded trains and buses, road tolls, traffic queues and the inconvenience of not having a train or bus station or car park nearby. If you are running your business from home you can almost fall out of bed and straight into work!

This means that over the years you save a significant amount of **wasted commuting time**, time which can be better utilised. For example, you may use the time saved each day to go for a walk or visit the gym, thereby **improving your health**. Some form of exercise sets you up for the day and energises you for the tasks ahead. It also gives you some valuable **thinking time** in which to plan how you are going to take your home business forward.

Reduced running costs

A significant advantage to running a business from home is that it **keeps your costs down**. In the early days it is vital to keep costs as low as possible, to maximise your chances of making a profit. Running your business from home means you will save rent on leased business premises, travelling expenses and other business costs such as rates.

Running your business from home may also mean that you are more productive than you would be if you worked in an office with other people.

The lack of distractions, such as meetings and passing the time of day with colleagues, means that you are able to focus on work. Another major advantage home businesses have over larger businesses is what might be called **business flexibility**. Home businesses can often move quickly to take advantage of **new technology and trends** giving them a competitive advantage over larger businesses, which are often slower to adapt.

Independence

You now make all the decisions, whether they are financial, budgetary, time management or strategic decisions. This may be viewed as an advantage or disadvantage (depending on the type of person you are). If you previously worked for an organisation many of these decisions may have been made for you, sometimes without you even knowing.

However, now that you are running your own business you will be making all the decisions to do with your business, including its aims and goals, how much will be spent on marketing and at what level the budget will be set.

Disadvantages

Separating work and family time

When running a business from home it is difficult to **separate work time from family time**. It can be very hard for children to understand why you cannot play with them if you are at home.

TIP: Before you start your business, make sure that everyone in your family understands how things will work and ensure that you have their full support. You will then need to maintain the personal discipline required to carry this through.

It can be a great help if you have a defined, separate space within your home where you will operate from. Family members will recognise that this is your **work space** and that when you are there you need to be left alone to get on with running your business.

Lack of social contact

Another disadvantage people find when running a business from home is the **lack of social contact**. If you have been used to working in a large office or factory, with lots of people around you, it can be difficult to adapt to working on your own.

You discover that you no longer have anyone to bounce ideas off or just interact with socially. This can lead to a sense of loneliness and isolation. Interacting with your customers is different to interacting with friends and colleagues in the workplace. If you are a really social person you may find that running a business on your own from home is not for you.

Lack of support staff

One significant issue to consider if you are thinking of starting a home business is the **lack of support staff**. You may have previously worked for a large organisation with in-house staff providing secretarial, IT, human resources, accounting and marketing support. If your computer or your printer broke down, someone would come to fix it for you.

When running your own business from home you will not have that level of support. These are functions for which you will now have to take primary responsibility and may even have to perform yourself or contract out. This can sometimes be a difficult adjustment to make.

Financial considerations

Budget perspective

If you opt for self-employment in your own home business, you will no longer receive a regular pay cheque. This is probably the biggest hurdle to face when trying to decide whether or not to set up on your own. It is an important issue and one which requires careful thought and planning, both from a financial and a personal perspective.

In deciding whether or not you can afford to take this step, you need to first work out **how much you need to pay yourself** to meet all your annual personal expenses including home loan payments, council rates, strata levies, utilities bills, food and general living expenses.

Remember that the figure for your salary will be **before tax**. You will therefore need to 'gross up' the figure you have arrived at for your personal expenses by your expected marginal rate of tax, to obtain the pre-tax figure for your budget.

For example, if you need to receive $50,000 a year to meet all your expenses, and you expect your marginal rate of tax to average out at around 25%, then you will need to earn around $67,000 before tax. If you pay 25% tax on $67,000 (around $17,000), the net amount you are left with is $50,000. If you were to budget for only $50,000 then you would only be left with $37,500 after tax which would not be enough to cover all of your personal outgoings.

If the budget that you prepare for your business (see pages 31 to 33) shows that it will be able to pay you that much and still make a profit, then all you have to do is achieve the budget!

Personal perspective

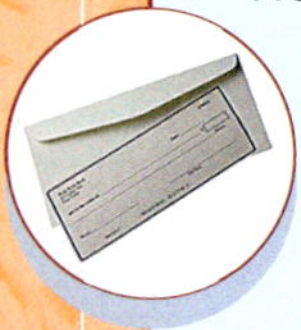

From a **personal perspective**, the lack of a regular pay cheque can raise a number of potential issues which you will need to think about before embarking on your business venture. Firstly, you will need to consider that even though you have budgeted for your salary, there may be times when the business cash flow **does not allow for a payment** to you. While customers may owe a lot of money to your business, that is not the same as cash in the bank.

Until you collect in some of that outstanding money, you may have to postpone paying yourself in order to have sufficient cash to meet other ongoing business expenses such as purchase of stock, or payment of electricity or telephone bills. Your pay cheque may **become irregular** and this could have an **emotional impact** on you. If you are unable to pay some of your personal expenses, this will undoubtedly result in stress for you (and your family) and you need to be prepared for that.

As your home business grows however, hopefully its cash flow will be at a sufficiently strong level that paying yourself regularly will not be a problem. In the early days of your business though, it is a definite possibility. You need to think about that and be **prepared to take that 'risk'** in light of the advantages and benefits running your own business can bring.

Do you have the temperament to live with that level of financial uncertainty and risk? Remember also that this 'risk' is one which is **shared by your family** so talk to them about the possibility and obtain their commitment to your business venture before setting out.

In addition you need skills in communication, negotiation, finance and organisational ability and have drive, determination, energy and vision.

Remember, you will be your own boss and set your own goals and rules. If you find it difficult to motivate yourself now, will the situation improve when you are your own 'whipcracker'?

The important thing is **not to over-emphasise the advantages nor to be put off by the disadvantages**, but to carefully weigh up both sides of the argument before deciding whether or not running your own home business is for you.

TIP

Since your final decision will be determined very much by your own personality and your personal goals, you may find it helpful to jot down what you personally see as the pluses and minuses of running your own home business. If the pluses outweigh the minuses then you can be re-assured that you are making the right decision for you.

TURNING YOUR IDEA INTO A BUSINESS PLAN

Every new business has to start somewhere and 'the idea' is always the **starting point.** You have thought of a product or service which you believe you can turn into a successful business. Often, this idea emerges out of a **hobby or interest.**

TIP

Remember that you intend to be running your own business for a very long time – perhaps the rest of your life. It is important that you enjoy what you do. You will be better at it and your chances of success will multiply. Otherwise, work will become a chore and you will lose interest.

Developing your Business Plan

Without doubt, planning is the most important aspect of setting up and running your home business. The **Business Plan** will be your guide as you begin to bring your idea to life.

To attempt to set up a business without a plan is a bit like visiting a foreign country for a driving holiday without taking a map with you. You will not clearly see where you want to go, how you are going to get there and whether you have sufficient resources to reach your destination.

This would be a foolhardy thing to do. The same principle applies when setting up your home business.

Business Plan checklist

The following Business Plan checklist is not exhaustive and not all of the points will apply equally to every business. However, it is a framework around which you can develop a plan for **your business.**

As you develop the plan, it will help crystallise some of the issues most vital to the success of your business.

Business Plan checklist

☑ Step 1 – Clarify your vision and goals

- ☐ What is your vision for your business?
- ☐ What are the motivations which are driving you to set up your business?
- ☐ What are your goals? (Set yourself 'smart' goals – **S**pecific, **M**easurable, **A**chievable, **R**ealistic, **T**imely)

☑ Step 2 – Refine your idea and your market

- ☐ What is your product or service?
- ☐ Who and where is your target market?
- ☐ Who is your competition? What do they charge?
- ☐ What is your competitive advantage? What makes your product or service sufficiently different from the competition to make customers favour it over others?
- ☐ How will you use advertising and promotion to get the message out to your target market?

☑ Step 3 – Plan your distribution strategy/website

- ☐ How will you deliver your product or service to your customers? Will you do it face to face, over the Internet or through a network of suppliers?
- ☐ Consider developing a business website.

☑ Step 4 – Assess what physical/human resources are needed

- ☐ What experience or skills do you have in the line of business you are establishing? What further training will you need?
- ☐ What additional human resources will you need, such as a partner, casual staff or external contractors?
- ☐ What equipment will you need?

☑ Step 5 – Investigate whether the business is financially feasible

- ☐ What financial resources do you have? Have you got capital or cash which you can use to start up the business or will you need to borrow money? Are you able to raise finance if required?
- ☐ How have you calculated your pricing? How does it compare with your competitors?

- ☐ What will be your profitability? How much profit will you make on each sale? Have you prepared a budget?
- ☐ What is your breakeven? How much profit do you need to cover your overheads?
- ☐ What are your financial projections, in particular your cash flow forecast allowing for credit given/taken?

☑ Step 6 – Conduct a SWOT analysis of your business

- ☐ **S**trengths
- ☐ **W**eaknesses
- ☐ **O**pportunities
- ☐ **T**hreats

☑ Step 7 – Select your business structure

- ☐ What will be your business structure – sole trader, partnership or company?

CLARIFYING YOUR VISION AND GOALS

Step 1 of your Business Plan involves clarifying your vision for your home business as well as the goals you have for your business.

Why have a vision?

It is very important that you have a vision for your business — a forward-looking view of where you want it to be in around five years time. Perhaps the focus of your vision is how you want to run your business. The emphasis here is on the **'big picture'** rather than specific goals.

While the idea of having a vision for your business might seem a bit 'airy-fairy', having a vision is about **what you want to achieve** by running your own business. Never lose sight of your vision and regularly remind yourself of it.

Here are some **tools** which can help you formulate your vision.

To begin with, try writing down some responses to the following questions in terms of: 1. Where you are now and 2. Where you want to get to:

- **Workload** – Your personal workload aims.
- **Location of your business** – You are thinking of running your business from home but will this still apply in the future?
- The **range of products and services** you will offer.
- What are your marketplace and potential customers?
- Your **motivations** for setting up and running your own home business.
- **How big** do you want your business to grow?
- What will your eventual **exit strategy** be – sale of the business, hand over to family member etc?
- Your broad **financial aims**.

By honestly answering the above questions, you will start to clarify the vision you have for your business.

Clarifying your goals

Your goals are the **building blocks** which support the vision. They are the steps which, if successfully implemented, will enable the vision to be achieved.

Start each day by reading your business goals. This will keep you focused on the things which are important to the success of your business.

It is essential to ensure that your goals are what are sometimes called 'SMART' goals, that is they should be:

- **S**pecific
- **M**easurable
- **A**chievable
- **R**ealistic
- **T**imely

For example, when formulating a goal for your annual sales, ensure you put down not only the **dollar figure** but also the **date** by which you want to achieve that figure.

Be realistic in your expectations and time frame. For example, don't overestimate your earnings in the short term. Write down your goals and then review them regularly. You may have achieved one goal and now need to set yourself a fresh one or you may have discovered that a goal is no longer achievable.

Remember also that it is vital you monitor your goals. There is absolutely no point in setting goals and then not measuring them, because you will never know if you have ever actually achieved them!

Your business goals will be highly influenced by the original motivations which drove you to set up your business in the first place, for example independence, a passion for your product or service, a need for better work/life balance, financial gain, or ageism in the workplace.

The areas in which you need to set goals include:

- **Financial** – What level of profit do you want to make? What do you want the value of your business to be?
- **Marketing** – How many customers do you want? What level of annual sales or fees do you want to achieve? How many products or services do you want to offer?
- **Operation**s – What skills do you need to buy in? What equipment do you need?
- **Personal –** What salary do you want to achieve from your business? What personal possessions do you want to be able to afford? How much time do you want to spend with your family?

MARKETING YOUR BUSINESS IDEA

Marketing is based on the concept that the **customer is the most important person** to a business. If you don't have any customers, you don't have a business! Marketing is all about creating a product or service which **customers want**, at the **right price**, **delivered to them** in the right way at an **acceptable profit** for your business.

The four 'P's

Traditionally marketing is based around what is called the '**four P's**'. These are:

- **P**roduct
  - Product or service range, breadth and mix
  - Product or service features and benefits
  - Product quality
  - Packaging
- **P**rice
  - Price levels
  - Price strategies
  - Credit terms (i.e. how long your customers have to pay)
- **P**romotion
  - Advertising (how much you will spend, what form of advertising you will use)
  - Publicity
  - Sales promotion (e.g. special offers)
- **P**lace
  - Distribution channels
  - Stock levels
  - Delivery

The 'four P's' form what is called the **Marketing Plan** which will comprise the basis of the marketing of your business. Think of them as ingredients in a cake. To bake a good cake, you need to include the ingredients in differing quantities, but all are necessary to achieve a successful outcome.

Developing a marketing plan

Refine your idea

Analyse your idea so that you are able to **clearly define** it. For example, you may want to set up a secretarial services business or alternatively an Internet-based business. Try to **be specific** about what you want to do and avoid trying to provide too many products or services, otherwise it will be difficult to focus and your business will lose direction.

Be clear about the market **demographic** you are targeting. In other words, what is the sex, age group, earning capacity etc of your market?

Carry out market research

The second step is to find out if there is a market for your idea. The need to research your potential market is **common to all types of businesses** from major banks to the local corner store.

There are two options available to obtain market research information:

1. Internal market research
2. External market research.

Internal market research normally involves using a business' own staff to 'test' new products or services and carry out market research.

Clearly, this is not feasible for a home business. At this level, internal research might involve you:

- talking to family and friends
- questioning respondents via mail or telephone
- hosting 'focus groups' in which invited people are asked questions about your proposed product or service.

The main advantage of carrying out market research yourself is that you can control the research process and adapt it to changing circumstances as you go along. For example, if you receive a poor response rate to a mailing campaign, you can quickly switch to something else.

TIP

By personally interviewing people, you gain a much deeper understanding of their responses through observation of their body language. They might say 'yes' to your question while their body language indicates they are lukewarm rather than really enthusiastic. You can also redirect your questioning to gain a clearer understanding or explore new topics.

You will need to **develop a questionnaire** setting out the questions you need answered in order to determine whether there is a demand for your product or service. Make your questions as **specific as possible** otherwise you are likely to end up with widely differing, vague answers which will not be of much use.

Restrict the number of questions to a reasonable level otherwise people will get bored and may answer without really thinking about their responses. Test out the questionnaire on family or friends first and refine it based on their responses.

External market research usually involves employing a market research agency or consultant to carry out the research for you or making use of information from publicly-available sources.

Employing an external market research agency can have a number of advantages. Firstly, it gives you access to **trained market researchers** who can help formulate the right questions for your questionnaire and provide advice on the most **cost-effective strategies** for collecting the information you need.

Secondly, agencies are often able to access a **much wider population** than you could ever hope to by doing the market research yourself. This enables you to focus your product or service in areas which will bring you the greatest opportunity for success.

You can find the names and addresses for market research agencies in your area by looking in the *Yellow Pages* or on the Internet at www.yellowpages.com.au. Alternatively try **searching the Internet** by using a search engine such as Google (www.google.com.au). Remember to refine the search criteria to your local area otherwise you may end up with agencies from around the world!

Employing an external research agency has **potential disadvantages**. The first is cost, although agencies often offer different levels of support at different costs. Ask what 'package' might suit you best in terms of quality research at a reasonable cost.

As well, by using external researchers you **lose some measure of control** over the interview process. As noted earlier, when you personally interview people you gain a much deeper understanding of their feelings because you can **observe** their responses as well as **hear** them. You can also redirect questioning where appropriate. External agencies will often simply collect the responses to the specific questions you want them to ask.

Information from publicly-available sources is also an option. The Australian Bureau of Statistics (www.abs.gov.au), for example, has free information on the economy, population profiles, regional trends, the environment and energy. If you don't have Internet access, try your local library.

TIP

Take notice of feedback and be adaptable in your thinking. This will enable you to change your ideas in line with market conditions. An awareness of what is happening in the marketplace and the ability to adapt accordingly is a vital aspect of any business.

Check out the competition

Investigate whether anyone else is already offering the same product or service. If they are, consider how you can make your product or service different so that customers will purchase from you rather than the competition. This is called a **differentiation strategy**.

For example, you might be able to offer a more personalised service or respond more quickly to your customer's needs being a smaller, more flexible business. Alternatively, your product might offer more features than others.

Be very careful if the only difference you can offer is price. Adopting a low-cost strategy makes your business extremely vulnerable to price changes. Your competitors may be able to reduce their prices below yours and, if low cost is your only selling point, you will be forced to reduce your prices even further.

This process could go on and on until one of you finds that you cannot reduce the price any further and has to wind up the business. This is a **very weak strategy** upon which to risk your whole livelihood. Instead, strive to provide a product or service which is **intrinsically different** in some way from the competition.

Advertising strategies

Another important element to consider is **advertising**. Think about how you will make potential customers aware that you have a product or service which they may want to purchase. This may, for example, involve direct advertising in newspapers, periodicals, direct mail or even radio or television.

Another way of advertising directly to your potential customers is through the Internet **via your own website**. However, do not undertake the expense of having a website unless it is likely to bring in new business.

A further way of advertising might be **networking** through face-to-face contact. This would involve joining organisations such as the Chamber of Commerce and business clubs, mingling with other members and handing out your business card.

TIP: Networking can be a powerful form of advertising because people get to meet you in person, and if they like you, they are more likely to make use of your products or services.

TIP: When designing your business card for your new home business, place your business name and contact details on the front of the card and include brief details of the products or services you are offering on the reverse side of the card. It will help people who receive your card to remember what it is you are offering.

Types of advertising

Let's have a closer look at the different **types of advertising** you might use, together with their respective advantages and disadvantages.

You do not have to just stick with one type of advertising – you can change your advertising mix as you feel appropriate. The important thing is that your overall advertising is effective.

Newspapers and periodicals

Advertising in newspapers or periodicals can be an effective way of **reaching a large number of people, relatively inexpensively**. You may decide to simply take out an advert in a newspaper or periodical, or you might incorporate an advert into a news story about your business in your local newspaper. Bear in mind that your story must have an 'angle' of some description to make it **newsworthy**.

If you decide to advertise in a magazine or industry publication, you might just take out an advert. Alternatively, you (or someone you employ for the task) could **write an article** which includes information about your product or service. For example, if you are providing interior decorating advice you might write in an interior decorating magazine about the latest trends in colour schemes and include details of your business.

In doing this, you are not only **publicising your expertise**, your article is likely to be read by people considering having some interior decorating done in their home. You are targeting the specific market you want to reach.

The **key questions** to ask before undertaking newspaper or periodical advertising are:

- What is the **circulation** of the newspaper or periodical — i.e. how many people does it reach?
- What **age group** is the newspaper or periodical aimed at? There is no point in advertising zimmer frames in a teenager's magazine!
- What is the **geographical spread** of the newspaper or periodical? Does it just cover the local area, or is it regional or national in its distribution?
- What is the **target market** of the newspaper or periodical? Remember the interior decorating example used earlier. There is little point writing an interior decorating article and then trying to publish it in a journal aimed at a different audience!

Direct mail

Direct mail is a relatively low cost option for home businesses. It involves obtaining an address list of potential customers and sending them a brochure advertising your product or service, either by post or via letter box drop.

If your target market is the general public, you could have an advertising leaflet printed and post them in letterboxes yourself. However, respect people's wishes. If there is a sign on the box saying 'No Advertising Material' then don't put one of your leaflets in!

For **more targeted advertising** you could draw up a list of potential customers yourself by trawling through publications such as the *Yellow Pages* to find businesses which might use your product or service. For example, if you were selling car wash supplies you could make a list of all the car wash operators in your area and send out your brochure to them.

Alternatively, you could **purchase a mailing list** from an external supplier. (They are listed in the *Yellow Pages* or may be found via an Internet search.) Talk to them about your target market to obtain a list relevant to your needs. For example, if you are providing IT support services to small and micro businesses ensure that the list contains names of businesses with fewer than say five employees.

Radio

Although it costs more, radio advertising provides you with the potential to **reach a greater number of people** than through newspaper or periodical advertising. Just consider the geographical range of radio stations and the number of people living within that range.

Radio advertising also has **some additional advantages**. For example, if you conduct a radio advertising campaign for your web page design service, the name of your business or the 'jingle' used in the advert will probably get stored in listeners' memories. Then, when they need a web page designed, your name or jingle is likely to pop up in their minds.

The main **disadvantage** of radio advertising over newspapers and periodicals is **cost**. To be really effective, radio advertising needs to be repeated time and again and ideally include a catch-phrase or jingle. The radio station will help you create the advert, but obviously that will be relatively expensive – as will be the need for the repeated slots on the station.

The message used in radio advertising needs to be **a simple one**. The format does not lend itself to complex advertising with long product lists or explanations of complex concepts.

The **key questions** to ask before undertaking radio advertising are:

- How many people listen to the radio station? Stations should be able to provide you with this information.
- What age group is the radio station aimed at?
- What type of listeners is the radio station trying to attract? For example, if your product or service is related to investments it might be advantageous to approach a radio station which plays classical music, as their listeners are more likely to have spare funds to invest.

Television

Television advertising can be an extremely effective way of promoting your product or service. The number of people you can reach via this form of advertising **can be huge**. Some television programs have viewers in the millions!

Another advantage is that you are better able to get across a relatively **complex message** more easily using television advertising than is possible with radio advertising. This is because you can use pictures as well as sound to communicate the message.

TIP: Research shows that people absorb visual information more effectively than information they can only hear. Therefore, a television advert can have a greater impact than a radio advert.

The main **disadvantage** of television advertising is **cost**. To create a television advert requires a team of people to produce, direct and possibly act in it. The television company will be able to help you with this. Different time slots on television have different costs.

For example, an advertising slot in the middle of a prime-time program will cost significantly more than an advertising slot during a non prime-time program later in the evening or after midnight.

TIP: Monitor the effectiveness of your advertising to maximise the return on your investment. This allows you to change your advertising strategy if necessary. For example, if you place an advert in a newspaper and get no responses you can try something different.

Weigh up the **costs versus the benefits** of all the options for advertising. There is little point in incurring the expense of a particular type of advertising (e.g. radio or newspaper) if it does not attract new customers.

Selling to intermediaries

Finally, if you intend to use **intermediaries** when distributing your product or service, consider how you will direct your advertising and marketing to them rather than the ultimate end-user of your product or service.

Fair trading

Remember also that advertising has to be fair and reasonable, and conform to the guidelines set out in the *Fair Trading Act* and the *Trade Practices Act*. For example, you are not permitted to promise something to a customer if you cannot deliver on that promise.

In addition, if there are **potential downsides** to your product or service then you must make potential customers aware of this. For example, if you are selling an investment which may fall in value as well as rise, then you must tell your potential customers this in your advertising.

Planning your distribution strategy

An essential part of successful planning for your business is to decide how you will distribute, or sell, your product or service to your customers. Your initial market research will have informed you how your competitors distribute their products or services and this will be a good indicator of how you should distribute yours.

For the average home business, using distribution channels **similar to your competitors** is a good starting point. Devising and establishing an entirely new way of distributing something which your competitors distribute in a way the market currently likes is a bold and risky move and often requires significant financial outlay.

TIP

There may be a different, better way of distributing a product or service but it takes time and money to change the deep-seated perceptions of customers.

How and where to sell your product

How will you sell your product or service to prospective customers? Will you **deal directly** with customers or will you use intermediaries to act as the 'middle man' in the transaction?

For example, if you want to sell a range of giftware then you will probably do this through **a shop or chain of shops**, rather than directly to the customer.

Where you choose to operate your business is often very important in terms of your distribution strategy. For example, if you plan to offer business computer support services, your customers are likely to be located in **central business districts.**

TIP: It is pointless operating your business a long distance away from your customers because the extra time and cost involved in service delivery could make your pricing uncompetitive, thus affecting the viability of your business.

MANAGING INFORMATION TECHNOLOGY AND DEVELOPING YOUR WEBSITE

Using information technology

In running a business from home it is important to realise that information technology (IT) (that is, your computer equipment) is **a resource you must have**, rather than something you would like to have.

You will use your computer to

- communicate with customers and suppliers (receiving and placing orders)
- maintain essential business records
- store and manage information about your customers
- research what is happening in your marketplace and the activities of your competitors.

Not too long ago, the idea of having a computer at home was thought to be beyond most people. Often the cost was prohibitive and the early computers were either too large or lacked the capacity to support a business. Thankfully, things have changed and it is now possible to obtain **powerful**, **small-scale computing equipment** at an affordable price.

While office supplies stores and specialist computer stores can advise you on the type of computer which best suits your needs, it is still a good idea to **carry out some research** before making a purchase.

For instance:

- Ask your computer-savvy friends about their equipment (e.g. its for instance: speed, memory and the type of software used).
- Consider the type of accounting software you intend to use and check the minimum computing requirements the package needs to run effectively.

Armed with this information you will be much better placed to identify the right computer to buy.

Managing your IT

It is important to have systems in place for managing your information technology. What happens if your computer crashes and all of your files are lost? Ensure that you **regularly back-up your important files** to a floppy disk, CD, zip disk or other storage device. Ideally these back-up files should be stored away from your premises in case of fire or burglary. If this is not possible, at least try to store your back-up files in a lockable, fire-proof cabinet.

Another important aspect of managing your IT is installing **virus protection** and **security against computer hackers** (people who can break into your computer via the Internet and steal or corrupt your data). A number of software packages are available which can protect you from such attacks and it is strongly advised that you not only install them on your computer but also ensure that they are **regularly updated.**

TIP: Be prepared for any of your IT equipment to fail, by ensuring appropriate support is in place. In the case of a home business this will often be an external IT consultant.

For the efficient operation of your business, you will need to have an Internet connection to send and receive emails and orders via your computer. What sort of connection you have will be determined by how much information you intend to communicate via the Internet.

If you think you will be communicating large files and lots of information then a **broadband connection** is recommended as this provides faster response times. If your usage is likely to be smaller in scale, then a simple **dial-up connection** will probably suffice. Dial-up is slower than broadband, but is often less expensive.

Since broadband connectivity is not yet available in some areas, you may have to use dial-up initially. Alternatively you might consider a **wireless connection** via a mobile phone signal.

Setting up a business website

With an **Internet-based business** you never actually meet your customers face to face. This type of business can be operated from virtually anywhere, so long as the necessary information technology and communications systems are available. (Of course, you don't need to be an Internet-based business to make use of a business website.)

TIP: A website can be used to attract new customers or to inform customers about your product or service as well as your vision for your business and your customer service ethics. Most importantly, it can enable customers to purchase your goods or services on-line.

The important thing to remember is that your website has to look good. One of the biggest hurdles facing a home-based business is portraying it to the outside world as a professional and credible business. A professionally designed website can go a long way to helping you meet this challenge.

Web-hosting services

Numerous companies providing **'web-hosting services'** will maintain your site for an annual fee. You can also purchase a domain name through the company (providing it is not already owned by someone else). For example, if you had an interior design business called **City Interior Designs**, it is likely that you would want your domain name to be something like www.cityinteriordesigns.com.au.

A web-hosting company can also help you with the **design and functionality** of your website. Often they have a number of reasonably priced and easy-to-use packages that allow you or the company to develop the site. These web design and development packages range from a few web pages featuring some basic information to full functionality providing your customers with the ability to purchase goods on-line via a secure payment facility.

'Search engine' deals

If you are already familiar with the Internet you will have used a 'search engine' such as Google, MSN, Sensis, Yahoo! or Ask Jeeves when looking for a particular topic. Search engine companies offer packages which ensure that when your potential customers conduct a search, your website is **among the first to be listed.**

To find companies providing the above services, look in the *Yellow Pages* under 'Internet Web Services' and compare prices and packages before making a choice.

ASSESSING YOUR SKILLS AND EQUIPMENT NEEDS

Personal assessment

When deciding to set up and run your own home business it is important to be honest with yourself about the areas where you have skills and those areas where you **need help**.

In all probability, you will already have experience in the line of business you intend to start up. For example, you might have decided to set up your own photography business since photography has been a longstanding hobby of yours.

However, running a successful business requires you to have other skills in addition to those related to the core activity of the business. For example you will need:

- **Communication skills** – to communicate effectively with customers and suppliers.
- **Organisational ability** – to organise your own time and that of any contractors you might employ.
- **Financial skills** – to manage the finances of your business.
- **Negotiation skills** – to effectively negotiate with customers and suppliers.

Before embarking on running your own business it is important to carry out a self-assessment of your abilities in all of the above areas. You might find it useful to score yourself out of 10 in each area. In this way you will be able to prioritise those areas where you need most help.

Once you have done this exercise, consider your weaker areas and how you might improve your skills in those areas. This might involve attending a **TAFE course** or a course run by your local college, Business Enterprise Centre or Chamber of Commerce.

Also have a look in your local book shop for books on small business management (see Further information on page 59).

Outsourcing

If you feel you cannot adequately address all of the gaps in your skills, and you do not want to take on a business partner or employ staff, you could consider outsourcing (contracting out) the role.

For example, if you have limited finance skills and do not want to employ a full or part-time bookkeeper, you might consider outsourcing the role to an external contractor or approaching your accountant for help.

Since an external contractor only works when they are needed, you gain the skills your business requires without unduly increasing your costs.

Equipment needs

When setting up your home business, it is important to think about what equipment you will need in order to be able to **operate effectively**.

As a starting point for a home business you should aim to have the following as a minimum:

- personal computer
- printer
- fax machine
- photocopier

In addition you will need **telephone equipment** including:

- a fixed telephone line (or perhaps two) for your fax machine and computer
- mobile telephone, so that your customers can reach you if you are away from your home office.

It is important for a home business to have a designated 'space' to operate from equipped with a desk, comfortable chair and filing cabinet.

You may also require specialist equipment such as:

- software (for example, an architect would require Computer Aided Design (CAD) software to produce drawings)
- manufacturing equipment (such as a lathe or drill)
- tools (for example, a furniture-making business would require woodworking tools).

Even though you are running a home business, you may need to visit customers from time to time. Will you need a **vehicle**? If you don't already have one, or if your family needs your existing vehicle to get to work or school, consider purchasing or leasing another vehicle.

If you don't want to use up your capital by purchasing a vehicle, consider **leasing** one instead. Leasing means that in effect you 'rent' the vehicle from a leasing company.

At the termination of the lease contract, you have the option of purchasing the vehicle for an agreed sum, or simply handing it back.

If you are trying to keep your initial costs down, which is always a good idea when first establishing a business, think about using public transport to get around to your customers or hiring a vehicle on the occasions when public transport is not a viable option.

IS YOUR BUSINESS IDEA FINANCIALLY FEASIBLE?

Once you have decided on your goals, what your product or service will be, how it will differ from the competition, what resources you will need, and how you will market and deliver it to your customers, you must find out whether your business idea is **financially feasible**.

To do this, you will need to calculate:

- what price you can sell your product or service for
- how much you are likely to sell over a year
- what the costs of running the business will be.

This is your feasibility study. In other words, you will need to **prepare a budget**.

Preparing a budget

In preparing a budget you will need to address the issues of:

- price
- volume
- running costs.

Price

TIP

You should aim to sell your product or service for the maximum amount possible, after checking out the price your competitors sell their product or service for and what customers will pay for your product or service.

Again, **market research** will be the key in determining the maximum price you can charge for your product or service. Ask people what they would be prepared to pay for your product or service and listen to their responses. Decide whether you will charge a similar amount as your competitors or whether your product or service is sufficiently different that customers would be prepared to **pay a premium** to purchase from you.

Volume

The next step is to consider how much of your product or service you can sell in a year. (A time frame of a year is a good starting place when preparing a budget.) Because some of the expenses you will incur, such as electricity and telephone, are generally payable quarterly and other expenses are monthly, it is easier at this stage to multiply everything out to a 12-month period.

Once you have completed your annual budget, you will need to prepare a **monthly budget**. (A specimen annual budget is provided on page 60.) Try to be realistic when considering how much of your product or service you can sell.

TIP: It is better to be slightly conservative in your budget estimates in case things don't go quite to plan. You can still set yourself a 'blue sky' target as well, to provide a stretching goal for yourself.

Costs of running the business

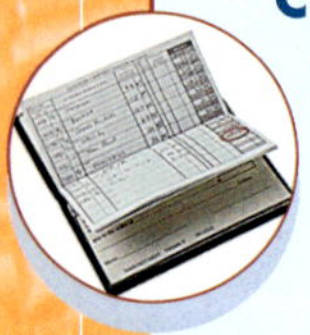

Once you have calculated how much of your product or service you can sell in a year, subtract the estimated annual costs of running the business (sometimes called **expenses, overheads or expenditure**). Whatever is left over is your **profit** (or **loss**, as the case may be).

TIP: When preparing the budget remember to include a salary for yourself, at whatever level you need to meet your personal expenses, such as home loan payments, council taxes, strata levies, food and general living expenses.

Remember that the figure you include in your budget for your salary will be **before tax. You will therefore** need to 'gross up' the figure you have arrived at for your personal expenses by your expected marginal rate of tax, to obtain the pre-tax figure for your budget. See page 9 for an example of how to calculate this.

If, after preparing the budget, you end up with a **profit**, think about how big that profit is. If it is only a small amount then any minor change in your income or your expenditure could **wipe out that profit** and turn it into a **loss**.

TIP: How might you be able to increase the volumes you can sell or the price you can sell for, or how might you cut back your expenditure, so that the profit figure is as big as you can make it? This will provide you with a good 'feel' for the level of risk you are taking on.

Profit and risk

The lower the profit the higher the risk and, conversely, the higher the profit the lower the risk.

If, after completing your budget, you end up with a loss then you have to seriously **rethink your business idea** and look for ways to turn that loss into a profit. Running your business from home rather than renting an office can help keep your expenses down by **saving on rent.**

TIP: Remember to be realistic in your budget and if possible overestimate your expenditure and underestimate your income a little so that you have a contingency built in if your budget doesn't quite work out as planned.

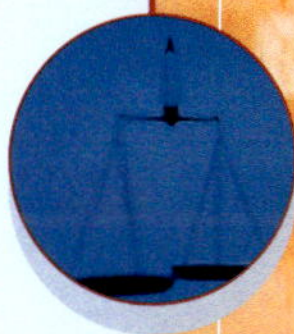

FINANCING YOUR HOME BUSINESS

Once you have established through your budget calculations that your business is financially viable, consider how you will **finance your new business.** This issue is often overlooked by people setting up their own business. However, finance is one of the most vital elements in setting up and running your new home business.

You need to consider:

- **establishment capital** – the amount of capital you will need just to set the business up
- **working capital** – the amount of capital you will need to keep your business running.

Sources of finance

Where will this capital come from? Will it come from savings, a redundancy payment or borrowing from family or a bank?

Try not to borrow money in the first two years after setting up your business. The business will have enough cash flow pressures to cope with without taking on the additional pressure of having to meet loan repayments. Banks will not allow you to miss scheduled repayments and this ongoing demand could seriously jeopardise your business.

Borrowing from family is a slightly better option because they will usually allow you greater flexibility in making repayments. However, as a general rule, it is recommended that you **try not to borrow money in the first two years of operation.**

If you do decide to borrow money from a bank, it is highly unlikely that you will obtain a reasonably substantial loan without providing security of some form, usually a mortgage over your home.

You need to give very careful thought before taking this step because if the business ultimately fails, the bank has the right to repossess your property and sell it to repay the loan.

Your spouse or partner will need to enter into the mortgage agreement and it is absolutely vital that you are both aware of the possible consequences of taking this step.

TIP

One advantage of using your home as security is that your loan will be at a much reduced interest rate compared to an unsecured loan.

Before you decide to use your property as security you should **seek the advice of your solicitor.** In fact, most banks now insist that you do this because they recognise the seriousness of the issue.

Establishment capital

Establishment capital is the money you will need to set up your business including the cost of machinery, equipment, stationery, accounting software and your salary.

Machinery, equipment and office stationery

The following list details just some of the items which might be included in your list of requirements:

- registration of your business name
- computer
- telephone
- mobile telephone
- fax machine
- website
- car or van
- specialist equipment if your business is manufacturing something
- desk and chair
- insurance
- initial stock
- fit-out of premises
- business cards
- stationery with your business name and address
- advertising leaflets.

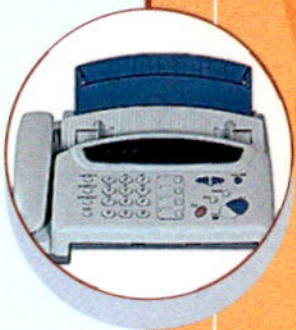

Accounting software

It is important that you set up some form of **record keeping and accounting system**, to keep track of cash, receipts, payments, stock levels, profitability and for tax purposes. There are various brands of reasonably priced software available from office supplies retailers, such as MYOB, Sage or Quicken.

Alternatively, a free package called E-record is available from the Australian Taxation Office.

Salary

Finally, you need to build into your calculation of establishment capital the amount of salary (plus tax) you will require to meet all your personal commitments (such as mortgage payments and living expenses) for the first 12 months of your new business.

If the business only generates enough income to cover its trading expenses then it may not be able to afford to pay you the wage you need to meet all your personal commitments. It is therefore important that you have sufficient capital to meet those commitments held in reserve, just in case.

Working capital

This is the amount of money you will need to keep the business running. Businesses have what is called an **operating cycle**. This means that you start out with cash. You then use this cash to purchase or manufacture stock. Stock is then sold to your customers. When payment is received from your customers, you use that cash to purchase or manufacture more stock and the cycle starts over again.

The critical point is the **time lag** between purchasing or manufacturing stock and receiving payment from your customers. Working capital is the cash you will need to **cover that gap**, allowing you to pay the ongoing expenses of the business until you receive cash from your customers.

'Cash is King'

The following saying should be at the forefront of your mind at all times when you are running your business: 'Cash is King'. The main reason businesses fail is lack of cash, as opposed to lack of profit.

Profit is a **paper measure of** how much you make on a particular transaction. For example, you might sell a product or service for $100 which has cost you $50 to make, so your profit is $50. However, until you have **actually been paid by your customer,** you have nothing with which to pay your own bills and expenses.

This is why it is vital that you ensure your customers **pay you promptly**. The longer the period between you selling them your product or service and their actually paying you, the **greater amount of working capital** you will need to finance the ongoing expenses of your business.

Cash flow forecast

To calculate how much working capital you will need you will need to prepare a cash flow forecast. (An example is provided on page 61.)

Using a spreadsheet is an ideal way to prepare your forecast because all the calculations are automatically performed by the computer program. This saves a huge amount of time when you want to run 'What If?' scenarios. Individual figures and the end result are automatically adjusted as you feed in various possibilities.

One of the **key assumptions** to feed into your forecast is the time period you will allow your customers to pay you and the time period your suppliers will allow you to pay them. While you may sell something today to a customer on 30-day credit terms, that customer may take more than 30 days to pay you.

You therefore need to **build these types of possibilities** into your cash flow forecast to determine how much working capital you will need to get you through until payment is received.

Suppliers are reluctant to provide long credit terms to new businesses so try to ensure that you keep the credit terms you offer your customers to a minimum.

Let's look at a couple of examples which highlight the importance of getting this aspect of your business right.

Example 1

Business A receives 30-day credit terms from its suppliers and offers 90-day credit terms to its customers. The business will have to pay out cash for its initial stock at least 60 days before it is due to receive any cash itself.

In addition, if it purchases a further amount of stock, it will also have to pay for this before receiving any payment at all from its customers. The cash flow of this business has to allow for the cost of at least two purchases of stock in estimating its required working capital. This will almost certainly put its cash flow under pressure from the very outset.

Example 2

Business B receives 30-day credit terms from its suppliers and offers 15-day credit terms to its customers. The business has cash coming in from its customers before it has to pay cash out to its suppliers and thus is in a much stronger position cash-wise.

Your cash flow forecast will show you what your working capital requirements are. The forecast bank balance will be either positive or negative. A **negative position** has to be covered by either borrowing from a bank or family or by an injection of capital by you into the business.

TIP

It is recommended that you run various 'What If?' scenarios in developing your cash flow forecast so that you can see what the worst case scenario looks like. If you base your cash flow requirements on this worst scenario, you will always have a safety net.

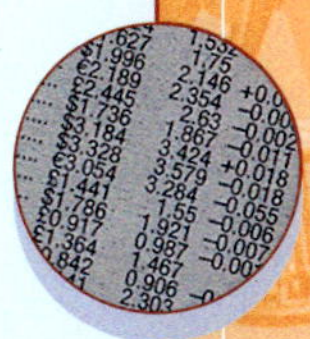

CHOOSING YOUR BUSINESS STRUCTURE

Once you have established that your idea for a home business is feasible and that you have sufficient finance to establish the business and run it, you can then move forward to set up your business. The first thing you will have to decide is what structure (or legal form) your business will take. The most common are a **sole trader**, a **partnership** or a **proprietary limited company**.

All of these structures have advantages and disadvantages and we will look at each of these in turn. Some of these relate to taxation and it is important that you **seek professional advice** on these matters from a qualified accountant.

Forms of business

Sole trader

This is the simplest form of business entity. Essentially it means that you will be running a business for which you are solely responsible **as an individual**. You will be taxed as an individual and you will be personally liable for any debts the business incurs.

The **advantages** of being a sole trader include simplicity and low establishment costs. There may also be tax advantages due to the tax-free allowances individuals can utilise.

A **disadvantage** is that taxation may be higher than for a proprietary limited company, especially if you earn large profits. The main disadvantage, however, is the fact that you will be personally liable for any debts the business incurs. This means that should your business fail, your creditors can pursue you personally for money owing to them. This could involve the loss of your personal assets such as your home or car.

Partnership

A partnership involves two or more people joining together to set up and run a business. Usually they will draw up a **Partnership Agreement**, which will set out, amongst other things, how the business will be run, how profits will be distributed and the circumstances under which the partnership can be dissolved. It is vital that such an agreement is **drawn up at the outset**, to prevent disputes in the future. All partners are considered by law to be jointly and severally liable for the debts of the partnership.

The **advantages** of this business structure are that it is relatively simple compared to a proprietary limited company and the establishment costs are relatively low. Also, any losses from the partnership can be offset against other taxable income (if any) of the partners.

The **disadvantages** are that taxation is more complex than for a sole trader and all partners are jointly and severally liable for the debts of the partnership. This means that if the partnership fails, creditors can pursue all or any of the partners for the full amount owing to them, potentially resulting in the partners losing their personal assets. As well, if the partnership fails and one partner disappears, the remaining partner or partners are liable for the full debts of the partnership.

The main disadvantage of a partnership, however, is that if at some time in the future the partners cannot agree on how the business should be run it usually means the business will fail.

Proprietary Limited company

In this structure, one or more shareholders, or owners, set up a company to run the business. The company is a **separate legal entity** from the shareholders or owners.

The **advantage** is that this structure provides shareholders or owners with some protection in the event of the business failing (unlike a sole trader or partnership). However, they are not fully protected if they are proven to be negligent in their running of the business, to the detriment of creditors. In addition, where the business is expected to earn large profits, a proprietary limited company can offer some taxation advantages over a sole trader or partnership.

The **disadvantages** of this business structure are higher establishment costs than for a sole trader or partnership because the services of an accountant are required in setting up the company. In addition, fees are payable for registering the company with the **Australian Securities and Investments Commission (ASIC)**.

Ongoing costs are also higher because the company is required to submit a return to ASIC at least annually and pay an annual fee. (Details of these fees can be found on the ASIC website.)

ASIC also lay down **very strict guidelines for directors of companies** which must be followed at all times. Failure to do so can lead to heavy fines or imprisonment. A further disadvantage is that taxation issues can be complex and the services of an accountant will probably be required for tax matters. This adds further to the costs of running the business.

As a general guide, if your annual sales are likely to be less than $100,000 then a sole trader is probably the best structure to start with, because of its simplicity and lower costs.

Purchasing a franchise

Another option is to purchase a franchise. A franchise is where you, as the franchisee, are granted **the right to use the franchisor's name and systems**. For example, McDonalds is a franchise. McDonalds Corporation is the franchisor with the owner of the local McDonalds outlet being the franchisee.

Advantages and disadvantages

In return for the right to use its name and systems, the franchisor is usually paid **an initial sum plus a royalty**, which is a percentage of the annual sales of the business.

The **advantages** of a franchise are that the franchisor usually supplies marketing, training and operational support to the franchisee plus, of course, an established brand name. This helps people who have little or no experience in running a business, reducing the risk of the business failing.

The **disadvantages** of a franchise are that, to a certain degree, the business is not entirely your own. You are not completely free to run it as you decide and are obliged to operate it within guidelines set out by the franchisor.

Additionally, it can be more costly than establishing your own business because of the initial franchise fee and subsequent royalties which have to be paid to the franchisor.

The terms of the arrangement between the franchisor and franchisee are set out in a **Franchise Agreement** which you should have checked out by your solicitor before signing.

TIP

If you do decide to buy a franchise, ensure that the product or service being supplied is something you are genuinely interested in. For example, it is no good purchasing a photographic franchise if you don't know the first thing about photography or don't have a genuine interest in it.

Purchasing an existing business

As an alternative to setting up your own business, you may decide to **purchase an existing business**. If you do, it is wise to ensure that you obtain, at a minimum, the **last three years trading results** which have been confirmed by the company's accountant. These will show you how the business has been trading and any trends in the business. (Beware if sales have been declining in recent years. This may indicate that the product or service being provided by the business is becoming obsolete.)

Note: Declining sales may be a result of the existing owner's **lack of interest** through, for example, ill health. If this is the case, it need not necessarily be a negative sign — on the contrary, it may be an opportunity to acquire a sound underlying business. You should also do the following:

- Obtain a thorough **history of the business** and its owners, including credit checks on the owners and/or company.
- Ask for a **breakdown of the purchase price** being sought. For example, are you buying stock, goodwill, patents or a combination of these? If in doubt as to their value, consult an accountant to ensure that you do not over-pay for the business.
- Find out the **reasons** behind the present owner's desire to sell the business.
- Always remember that **if something sounds too good to be true, then it probably is**!

Administrative matters

Having chosen the form of your home business, there are a number of administrative matters you will need to attend to in setting it up.

Registration

If you intend to trade under any name other than your own, you will need to register that name with the **Australian Business Register**, which can be done via their website. You will receive an **Australian Business Number, (ABN)** which you must quote on all invoices you issue. Otherwise your customers will be required to withhold tax at the rate of 48.5% and pay this direct to the Australian Taxation Office (rate current as at writing).

If you are trading as a proprietary limited company you must also obtain an **Australian Company Number (ACN)**.

GST

If the annual turnover (sales) of your business is $50,000 or more then you need to **register for GST**. If your annual turnover is less than $50,000 then you are not required to register for GST, although you can do so voluntarily if you choose to (figures current as at writing).

Once you have registered for GST you must add GST at the prevailing rate to all your invoices. At regular intervals, either monthly or quarterly, you will be required to complete a **Business Activity Statement (BAS)** which summarises all the GST you have received and paid.

If you have received more GST than you have paid, you must send the amount owing to the Australian Taxation Office. If you have paid more GST than you have received, then the balance is payable to you by the Australian Taxation Office.

Accounting and taxation issues

Annual tax return

All businesses are required to submit an **annual tax return**. This details your taxable income for the year and the amount of tax due on that income. Amounts you have already paid during the year under Pay As You Go (PAYG) will then be deducted and the difference is either payable to the Australian Taxation Office or, if overpaid, will be refunded to you.

The Australian Tax Office provides excellent support to new businesses through free publications and its website. Tax laws change regularly so it is important to keep up-to-date with changes which may affect your business. Remember that ignorance of the law (or changes to the law) is not a valid excuse if you fall foul of the regulations.

Financial record keeping

You must keep **accurate records** of all costs and outgoings incurred in running your home business, both for accounting and taxation purposes. In order to be able to claim business expenses which you can offset against your business income for taxation purposes, the **Australian Taxation Office** requires you to justify the proportion of expenses which relate solely to your business activities, as distinct from your private expenditure.

For example, if you claim a percentage of your electricity bill as a **business expense** you must be able to demonstrate the accuracy of your claim. The best way to approach this is to dedicate a part of your home — a spare bedroom or the garage — solely for business use.

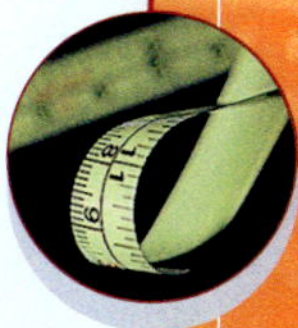

Estimate the amount of space your business occupies within your home in percentage terms and **claim expenses proportionately**. For example, if your office takes up 10% of the total floor space of your home, then a claim of 10% of your electricity bill and other utility bills (including GST) would not be unreasonable.

Ideally, the Australian Tax Office would prefer that you have separate meters and a separate telephone line for the part of your home used for business purposes. While a separate telephone line is relatively easy to arrange, the cost of installing separate meters may be prohibitive or impractical.

Whatever your approach to this issue, you must be able to clearly justify the proportion claimed. If you feel unable to do this then the Australian Taxation Office will allow you to claim **a fixed rate per hour**. In the tax year 2004/2005 this was 26 cents per hour.

You may also consider claiming a proportion of your **mortgage interest** or **rental payment** as a business expense, using the proportion method outlined above. However, bear in mind that if you do this you will probably **lose** a similar proportion of your **prime residence capital gains tax allowance**.

If you sell your home at a profit there is no capital gains tax on that profit. However, if you have been claiming a proportion of your mortgage interest as a business expense, at say 10%, then **10% of the profit** you make on the sale of your house may be subject to capital gains tax.

For more information on what you can and cannot claim, visit the Australian Taxation Office website on www.ato.gov.au or speak to your accountant. See also Blake's Go Guide *Small Business and Tax*.

Accounting and GST

You can choose one of two methods for accounting and GST purposes: cash accounting or accrual accounting. With **cash accounting** you only account for cash actually received or paid. For example, if you have issued an invoice but it has not been paid, you do not account for this amount. With **accrual accounting**, you account for all items, whether paid or not.

This can have quite significant implications for your cash flow. If you are accounting on an accrual basis, you may have to pay GST to the Australian Taxation Office for an invoice you have issued which has not yet been paid.

TIP

Generally speaking, for a small business the cash accounting method is the best one to adopt.

PAYG

Pay As You Go, or PAYG, is the mechanism by which taxation is reported and paid to the Australian Taxation Office. This may be tax due on business profits, called **PAYG Instalments**, or amounts you have deducted from payments you have made to suppliers or employees, called **PAYG Withholding**.

PAYG is detailed and remitted via the Business Activity Statement (BAS). More information on PAYG can be found on the Australian Tax Office website at www.ato.gov.au.

If you intend to employ staff, you will need to register this fact with the Australian Tax Office. It will then be necessary to:

- obtain information on **pay awards and health and safety regulations**
- establish **superannuation** arrangements
- take out **workers compensation** insurance.

For more information check out the websites listed on page 58. Companies providing **human resource services** can help you with employing and paying staff or contractors. For example, they can administer your payroll for you. This can sometimes be an administrative headache which you can do without, especially when you need to concentrate on generating sales and monitoring cash flow.

Business bank account

Your business will need a **separate bank account**, unless you are operating as a sole trader, in which case you can use your private bank account. However, it can get confusing if both private and business transactions are passed through the same account, so setting up a separate account for your business is recommended. The bank will need to see evidence of the trading name of the business as well as your ABN/ACN to open the account.

Shop around for the best package for your business. Most banks offer special fee arrangements for small businesses so compare them and decide which will be the best for you.

TIP: Choose a bank which is conveniently located, particularly if you need to deposit cash payments. Make sure it has car parking facilities so you don't have to carry cash over a long distance.

You will need a **cheque book** for your business and possibly the facility to receive credit card payments from your customers, if you are going to offer them that payment option.

Ask your bank for **statements of account** to be sent to you at least monthly, so that you can reconcile the account with your business records on a regular basis.

On-line (or Internet) banking is a very useful service which allows you to:

- view your account 24 hours a day
- print statements
- transfer money between your accounts
- make payments to third parties.

Once you are up and running, most of the paperwork for the business will probably need to be done in the evenings. The ability to view your bank account and carry out transactions outside normal office hours is thus extremely useful.

Insurance

It is important to **insure your business assets** including premises, contents, equipment and vehicles against loss, theft etc. You may also need to take out **public liability insurance** and **professional indemnity insurance** if you are providing professional advice to your customers.

Your normal home insurance policy will probably **not provide cover** for your home business equipment. For example, it will certainly not cover you for the loss of any stock stored at home. Similarly, your motor insurance policy will probably not cover use of your car for business purposes.

Advise your insurance company of your intention to run a business from home and ask them to issue an official notification confirming that they have been so advised. This ensures there can be no argument on this issue at a later date should you need to make a claim.

Don't forget the most important asset the business has — you. You should consider taking out insurance to protect your income in the event of ill health or accident. Remember that you no longer work for an employer who may continue to pay you if you have an extended period of sick leave.

Obtain quotes for your insurance needs from an **insurance broker** or through one of the number of specialist insurers for small businesses (see contact details on page 58).

Licences

Certain types of business (for example, the real estate and building and construction industries) require special licences to be able to operate. More information on licences can be found on the Government website at www.business.gov.au. If your business is required to have a licence to operate then you must obtain this before starting to trade.

Planning permission

You may require local council permission to operate your business from your home. **Planning schemes** administered by local councils often impose limitations on the use of residential premises for business purposes. It is advisable to check with your local council about the **zoning of your property** and whether or not you require a planning permit to operate your business from home.

ESSENTIAL BOOKKEEPING

Right from the first day your home business starts trading you will need to keep bookkeeping records of how your business is performing. A lot of people see the word 'bookkeeping', shudder with horror and call in the accountant! But it does not need to be that way. If you can complete a few **basic bookkeeping records** yourself, you will not only gain a greater understanding of your business, but also save yourself accountant's fees.

You need to keep **three main books or records** to maintain financial control of the business. They are:

1. cash book
2. sales ledger
3. purchases ledger.

TIP

You can purchase these books from office stationery suppliers at little cost. Alternatively you will find these bookkeeping functions in most of the accounting software packages mentioned in this Guide.

Cash book

The cash book is used to record the **payments and receipts** for your home business — that is, all the money going in and out of your business. It is usually divided into receipts on the left-hand side of the page and payments on the right-hand side.

Each page contains columns in which to record money passing in and out of your business. (The headings of these columns will be similar to those shown in the cash flow forecast example provided on page 61).

Receipts and payments should be added up each month. The total for the 'Bank' columns should equal the sum of the receipts and payments columns. **Total receipts, less total payments, should equal your business bank account balance.**

Deducting total payments from total receipts will give you the **net cash movement** for your business in that month. By adding this figure to your cash balance carried forward from the previous month, you will arrive at the new cash balance at the end of the current month.

This figure should then be compared to your bank statement to ensure that they match (allowing for any outstanding cheques). This process is called **reconciliation** and is a vital element in monitoring the performance of your business.

Sales ledger

The sales ledger (sometimes called the **debtors ledger**) is a record of all sales made.

You should record in the sales ledger:

- date of invoice
- amount of invoice
- customer's name,
- amount of GST (if applicable)
- date invoice was paid.

TIP

The date the invoice was paid is very important because it will enable you to quickly check at any time which customers have not yet paid and need to be 'chased up'. The date is also important because it will enable you at any time to quickly check how much you owe your suppliers (or creditors) and compare this figure to the amount of cash on hand to pay those invoices.

Purchase ledger

The purchase ledger (sometimes called the **creditors ledger**) is a record of all the goods and services you have purchased for your business.

This can include such items as:

- stock purchases
- telephone expenses
- stationery purchases.

Details which you should record in the purchase ledger include:

- date of invoice from the supplier
- amount of invoice
- supplier's name
- amount of GST (if applicable)
- date invoice was paid.

Keeping your records up-to-date

It can be difficult to find the time to keep your records up-to-date, given the day-to-day time pressures of running your business. However, since they are an essential part of the survival of your business, it is time well spent.

As a general rule, the cash book should be completed **daily** and the sales and purchase ledgers at least **weekly.** At the end of each **month** a reconciliation should be completed to ensure that your records are accurate and determine the cash position of the business. This is sometimes called **balancing the books**.

If the bookkeeping tasks are allowed to fall behind, it will take a long time to catch up and will become a real chore. By taking just a few minutes each day or week to make your entries, the job will seem a lot easier.

Having up-to-date, accurate records will save you time and money when the time comes to prepare the year-end accounts for your tax return.

Your business records will be invaluable if you ever receive a visit from the tax authorities. A set of up-to-date, accurate records will go a long way towards demonstrating that you are a serious business person.

Finally, it cannot be stressed enough that cash flow is probably the **most critical issue** which all businesses, including home businesses, face. It is especially critical for new businesses.

It is essential that you know exactly what your business' cash position is at all times. This will help ensure that your business does not run out of cash.

MANAGING THE 'BIG PICTURE'

You have now embarked on the journey of running your own home business. It is established and you are now trading. However, it is very easy in the early days to become side-tracked by the day-to-day issues that arise. It is important not to lose sight of the **planned goals and strategies** for your business for the longer term.

Research shows that many business people are **under time pressures**. As a result, some of the more important 'management' areas tend to get neglected. Beware! Neglecting these issues is a **recipe for disaster**. A balance has to be struck between the daily operation and the management of the business.

Management issues

Cash flow and debtor management

We have already discussed the importance of credit given and credit taken and the potential impact on the cash flow of your business. As you enter into the day-to-day running of your business it is very **easy to forget the importance of cash flow** because you are pre-occupied with sales, production, stock purchasing and so on. However, you ignore cash flow issues at your own peril. If not managed properly, it will be the undoing of your business.

Consider the **terms of payment** you are offering to your customers, being mindful of the terms you are receiving from your suppliers and the amount of cash needed to keep the business running.

TIP: It is not good business practice to offer extended payment terms to a customer just to get their business — it is no use 'buying' sales if you end up not getting paid by your customer. No amount of sales invoiced can replace actual cash received in terms of helping you pay your expenses.

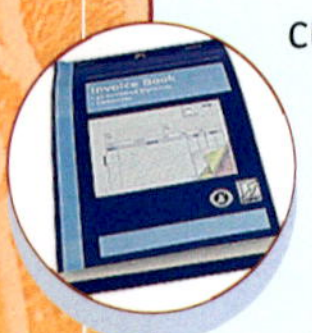

Monitor your debtors and creditors at all times. If one of your customers has not paid you in accordance with your agreed terms, do not put off taking action to ensure payment. Talk to your customer early about the non-payment to check whether it is just an oversight or if there is a problem.

While communication is vital in the collection of outstanding debts, if it gets to a stage where, despite promises, payment is still not forthcoming, consider stronger measures — perhaps hiring a debt collection agency.

Initially, a **letter from your solicitor** might bring about the desired result. If not, you may have to consider **legal action** for recovery of the money. However, this can be expensive and you should think long and hard before embarking on such a course. Try to deal only with those customers who are likely to pay you promptly for your product or service.

Customer service

This is an area which a lot of businesses neglect — to their cost! It is absolutely vital to **stay in touch with your customers**. Listen to what they have to say about your products or services, how you deliver them and how they feel about doing business with you.

TIP

Each of your customers needs to feel that they are your most important customer, because in their eyes they are! It is a truism that customers are often prepared to pay a little more for good service and if they receive it, they are more prepared to forgive any mistakes. These are vital factors in the success of your business.

Always remember that people **buy on emotions**. Some people will try to argue that they are entirely objective when they buy something, researching the product or service, checking out its features and comparing the cost to similar products or services. While it is true that they may do some or all of these things, ultimately they buy the product or service on emotion.

This may take the form of a **good feeling** about something: how grand it looks (in the case of a house), how fast it will go (in the case of a car), how well they look in it (in the case of clothing). The deciding factor in taking the step to purchase a product or service may simply be that the whole buying experience is **a pleasurable one**.

This involves making the whole process easy for the customer and making them feel valued. Remember — **a happy customer will come back** and buy from you again and again. Not only that, they will tell their friends about their experience, which is the **best form of advertising** you can have.

An important part of the customer service 'experience' is that you deliver your product or service **right first time, every time**. First impressions count and you do not get a second chance to make a good first impression. This may be influenced by your appearance and professionalism when meeting them for the first time or even how you answer the telephone.

When answering the telephone try to ensure that you are smiling. Your body language will positively affect the 'feeling' which you transmit down the line. Your customer will pick up on it and also react positively. Conversely, if you are downbeat, this too will be picked up by the customer.

Be aware that working from home can lead to a falling off in **dress standards**.

Always put yourself in the shoes of your customer. Think about how you would want to be treated if you were purchasing something from your business. How would the customer expect you to appear, given the type of business you are in? If you are running a secretarial business, your customers would reasonably expect you to be smartly dressed and businesslike. Turning up in shorts and tee-shirt would hardly give that impression!

Never be afraid to ask your customers what they think of your business and how they rate the service they receive from you. **Customer feedback** is arguably the most important piece of information you can receive. It will tell you what your customers like about doing business with you and what they dislike, providing you with the opportunity to improve where necessary. The feedback may even highlight areas where you had no idea there was a problem!

Managing strategy

Try to avoid becoming so immersed in the day-to-day running of your business that you lose sight of your longer-term strategy and goals. In other words, you need to **get off the dance floor and on to the balcony**!

It is so easy in the early days to be chasing sales and attempting to find new customers, or to become overly involved in the production side that you lose sight of the overall direction of your business. You may fail to give enough attention to the strategic part of owning and running a business.

It is a good idea to allow yourself some time each day to 'get up on the balcony'. This might take the form of going for a walk or a swim for perhaps 30 minutes a day. Not only will this be good for your personal health, it will also be good for the **health of your business**. Leave your mobile telephone at home and spend that time thinking about where you are with your business, where you want to be and how you are going to get there.

You might also use the time to think through some issues affecting your business in relation to finance, growth goals and the competition. It is amazing how productive and beneficial it can be when your mind is clear and able to focus on **important longer-term issues** rather than being overwhelmed by the day-to-day demands.

Monitoring performance

This is an area where a lot of businesses fall short, but which is vital in helping you understand how your business is performing.

Do you recall all that time spent preparing a business plan, budget and cash flow forecast for your business? So often businesses then **fail to monitor their actual performance** against those forecasts with the result that they fail to achieve their full potential or, even worse, the business collapses.

There is no point setting out business plans and then not **measuring your performance** against those plans. Monitoring actual performance against forecast performance enables you be an active manager of your business as well as to **foresee potential problems** and take corrective action.

Consider the following **scenario**:

You originally planned that your business would generate sales of $5000 per month or $60,000 per annum. Yet after three months trading you have only generated sales of $10,000. You note that this indicates you are $5000 behind your forecast for the 3-month period which, if continued unchecked, will equate to annual sales of $40,000 — some $20,000 less than you had forecast.

It is important to understand why this has happened and take **corrective action as early as possible.** It's no good waiting until the end of the year before finding that your earnings are down by $20,000. Monitoring your revenue position gives you the opportunity to do something about it. It may be that you have an order in hand which will bring your sales back in line with your forecast, or you may have to reassess your marketing strategy.

TIP

A vital element in monitoring performance is the regular reconciliation of your bank account. You should regularly reconcile your business expenses and sales receipts with money in and out of your account. That way you have a good idea of how the cash flow of your business is performing, which helps you avoid problems.

BUILDING A SUPPORT TEAM

As your business grows, you will need to build a **team of advisors** around you who can help and support you as your business moves forward. This team could include an accountant, a solicitor, a computer support person, a bank manager, a business coach/mentor and even fellow business people.

Your team members

Accountant

An accountant can help you **prepare your financial year-end accounts** and **advise on taxation/GST issues**, which are often very complex. The bookkeeping records which you will have kept will help your accountant tremendously by reducing the amount of time needed to compile your accounts. This not only saves you money in accountancy fees but also allows more time for discussing taxation strategies for your business.

An accountant can also help you with **company law** (if you are trading as a company) in relation to the completion of **annual accounts**, **filing of returns to ASIC** and generally complying with the various *Companies Acts*.

Solicitor

A solicitor can help you with **partnership law** if you are thinking of trading as a partnership. This can include advice on the legal position of partners and help in drawing up a **partnership agreement**, which is essential if you intend to trade as a partnership.

They can also help you by **scrutinising any contracts** you may be thinking of signing with potential customers, suppliers to your business, franchisors or other parties.

Hopefully you never become embroiled in **litigation** at any stage of your business, but if you do, the help and guidance of a solicitor will be absolutely vital because the issues and procedures can be extremely complex, and the costs of getting it wrong can be huge.

Involve your solicitor at as early a stage as possible if you see potential problems ahead. Don't do as the ostrich did and bury your head in the sand!

Bank manager

Building a relationship with your **bank manager** can be vital to maximising the chances of the bank supporting your business financially. For example, your business might need some short-term help to **pay expenses**, pending receipt of monies owing, or you may want to **expand the business** or **purchase new equipment**.

You will need the support of your bank manager and if they have seen your Business Plan, and have been kept informed of how the business is progressing, you are much more likely to receive the bank's support. Being able to provide up-to-date records of how the business is performing financially will also greatly assist.

Business coach or mentor

Having a business coach or mentor is a good idea, particularly in the early days. Setting up and running your own business can be a very lonely experience at times and having **someone to talk to about your business** and the challenges facing it can be extremely helpful.

You can also use them as a **'sounding board'** for any ideas you have for improvements.

Fellow business people

Networking with fellow business people allows you to share with others the day-to-day issues and problems you face in running your home business. In all likelihood they have already experienced the same issues and problems you are facing and can provide **valuable advice and support**.

TIP

Fellow business people may become future customers of yours once they know what it is you are selling. Getting to know such people may increase your sales as well as providing help and support.

There are a number of forums where business people can get together, relax a bit and discuss issues and problems. These include **Chambers of Commerce, Rotary clubs and small business and micro-business networking clubs**. You can usually find details of these organisations in your local press or on the Internet.

A FINAL WORD

In the early days of your home business, and indeed throughout the life of your business, you will encounter the **emotional rollercoaster**. There will be times of **personal stress** when you experience doubts about whether you did the right thing in setting up your business and feel like giving the whole thing up.

There will be times when you are worried by the fact that you don't have enough sales, and there will be times when you are worried because you have too many sales and are wondering how you are going to meet all your delivery deadlines! These are the **'dips'** on the emotional rollercoaster.

There will also be times of **great personal satisfaction**. Winning that big order you have been after for so long; receiving a letter or word of appreciation from one of your customers; or winning an award. These are the **'highs'** on the emotional rollercoaster.

Do not be too concerned by these 'dips' and 'highs' — these emotions are common to all owners of businesses and you are not the first to encounter them. **Take heart from this.** If you are aware that you will have some difficult times as well as some great times, you will be much better prepared to deal with them.

In conclusion, setting up and running your own home business is a journey. It offers you independence, the flexibility to manage the business around your lifestyle and, hopefully, financial reward.

If you remain **focused on the positive reasons** why you embarked on the journey in the first place, and keep a **careful eye on the potential pitfalls**, there is no reason why your home business should not be a great success. We hope that this Guide will help you in your journey.

FURTHER INFORMATION

Websites

www.abbi.com.au – Insurance information
www.abr.gov.au – Registration of ABNs
www.acci.asn.au – Australian Chamber of Commerce and Industry
www.asic.gov.au – Company information, company registration
www.ato.gov.au – Taxation, BAS, GST, accounting
www.ausindustry.gov.au – Range of incentives to support business innovation, small business services
www.beca.org.au – Business Enterprise Centres, advice on all aspects of starting up a business, links to local Business Enterprise Centres
www.business.gov.au – Setting up a business, licences
www.businessclub.com.au – Business planning
www.fca.com.au – Franchising Council of Australia, for assistance with franchising
www.grantslink.gov.au – Grants
www.homebusinessmanual.com.au – Covers a range of issues affecting home-based businesses
www.mbn.com.au – The Micro and Home Business Network program allows you to link up with other micro business owners in your local community and throughout Australia, showcase your product or services in expo's or win awards through its business award program.
www.nohsc.gov.au – Occupational health and safety issues
www.ozsmallbiz.net – Offers a range of support options
www.powerhomebiz.com – Home business resource web page
www.sbdc.com.au – Small Business Development Corporation, advice on starting a business, business support
www.smallbiz.nsw.gov.au – Advice on getting started in business, technology, Government support, training, managing a business, information for home-based businesses

Magazines

Mybusiness magazine www.mybusiness.com.au
DSB magazine www.loyaltyaust.com.au
Work from Home www.isubscribe.com.au

Books

Guerrilla Marketing for the Home-Based Business, Houghton Mifflin, 1995 by Jay Conrad Levinson

J.K. Lasser's TM Taxes Made Easy for Your Home-Based Business: The Ultimate Tax Handbook, Wiley, 2002 by Gary W. Carter

Keeping the Books: Basic Record Keeping and Accounting for the Successful Small Business, Dearborn, 2004 by Linda Pinson

Make Your Small Business Website Work: Easy Answers to Content, Navigation, and Design, Rockport Publishers, 2004 by John Heartfield

The Complete Idiot's Guide to Publishing Magazine Articles, Alpha Books, 2000 by Sheree Bykofsky, Jennifer Basye Sander, Lynne Rominger

The Successful Business Plan: Secrets & Strategies (4th edn) The Planning Shop, 2003 by Rhonda Abrams

Writing a Convincing Business Plan, Barron's, 2001 by Art DeThomas, William B Fredenberger and Lin Grensing-Pephal

Your Home Business: Insights, Strategies and Start-up Advice for Aspiring Entrepreneurs, Allen & Unwin, 2004 by Helen Chryssides

101 Ways to Advertise Your Business: Building a Successful Business with Smart Advertising, Allen & Unwin, 2004 by Andrew Griffiths

Other sources of information

Banks often have lots of information to assist small businesses. Some also produce free guides, available from branches or via their websites.

The Australian Tax Office (www.ato.gov.au) has published a series of free guides and tools to help small businesses.

EXAMPLE Budget

Income	
Sales (A)	
Cost of goods sold (B)*	
Gross Profit (A – B = C)	
Expenses	
Accountancy fees	
Advertising	
Bank charges	
Computer costs	
Electricity	
General expenses	
Hire of equipment	
Insurances	
Legal expenses	
Motor vehicle expenses	
Payroll tax	
Printing, stationery & postage	
Salaries	
Repairs & maintenance	
Contractors' fees	
Superannuation contributions	
Telephone	
Total Expenses (D)	
Net Profit (C – D)	

* Opening Stock, plus Purchases, minus Closing Stock

EXAMPLE Cash Flow Forecast

	Jan	Feb	Mar	Apr	May	Jun	Jul	Aug	Sept	Oct	Nov	Dec	Totals
Income (A)													
Sales/Fees revenue													
Payments													
Creditor payments													
GST payable													
Accountancy fees													
Advertising													
Bank charges													
Light/Heat/Power													
General expenses													
Insurances													
Motor expenses													
PAYG													
Postage/Stationery													
Salaries													
Superannuation													
Telephone													
HP/Lease /Loan payments													
Total Payments (B)													
Net Income/Payments (A-B=C)													
Opening Bank Balance (D)													
Closing Bank Balance (D+C)													

GLOSSARY

Accounting software Computer software packages which can help you complete the essential business records you need to keep.

Budget A financial plan for your business, setting out the expected sales income, the costs of running the business and the profit you hope to achieve.

Business Activity Statement (BAS) A monthly or quarterly statement to the Australian Tax Office which summarises all the GST you have received and paid. It only applies if you are registered for GST.

Business coach/mentor A person who can help you make your business more successful by sharing their business experience and skills with you.

Business plan A framework to help crystallise the key issues for the success of your business including your vision, goals and marketing and financial plans.

Cash book Used to record the receipts and payments for your business — that is, all the money going in and out of your business.

Cash flow Cash into and out of your business — probably the most important issue you need to consider when running a business.

Credit terms The amount of time which you allow your customers to pay you (and which your suppliers allow you to pay them).

Demographics Statistics relating to a particular group (your potential customers) e.g. where they live, their age group and how much they earn.

Differentiation strategy How you make your product or service different to that offered by your competitors so that customers will purchase from you.

Direct mail Advertising information mailed to a list of potential customers.

Establishment capital The amount of money required to set up your business including the cost of machinery, equipment, stationery, accounting software etc.

Information technology Computer equipment which will help you to gather, store and exchange information.

Marketing mix The various marketing strategies which are employed to your business' best advantage.

Market research Research carried out to establish if there is a market for your product or service and what that market's preferences are.

Networking Meeting with other business people to share knowledge and experiences and promote your business.

Outsourcing Contracting someone who is not an employee of your business to carry out tasks for you.

Overheads The general costs involved in running a business such as insurance, postage, electricity etc

Purchase ledger (creditors ledger) A record of all the goods and services you have purchased for your business.

Sales ledger (debtors ledger) A record of all your business sales.

'Smart' goals Targets you set for your business which are Simple, Measurable, Achievable, Realistic and Timely.

SWOT analysis An analysis of your business in which you consider its Strengths and Weaknesses as well as Opportunities and Threats.

Web-hosting service A company which will register, host and maintain your business website.

Working capital The amount of money required to keep your business running on a daily basis.

INDEX